GUITAR SHEETS
SONGWRITING

The Missing Method
An imprint of
Tenterhook Books, LLC
Akron, Ohio

Christian J. Triola

Discover what you've been missing.

Copyright ©2020 Christian J. Triola, Amy Joy Triola

All Rights Reserved.

Except as permitted under the U.S. Copyright Act of 1976, no part of this publication may be reproduced, distributed, or transmitted, in whole or in part, in any form or by any means, or stored in any form of retrieval system, without prior written consent of the author.

Bulk sales inquiries can be directed to the author at info@themissingmethod.com.

Cover and Book Design by Amy Joy, ©2020 Amy Joy

First Edition 2020, Tenterhook Books, LLC

Print ISBN-13: 978-1-953101-15-0

Table of Contents

Introduction i
Lyric Paper 1
Staff Paper 31
TAB Paper 83
Appendix 135
    Basic Chords 136
    Basic Scales 137
    Common Strum Patterns 138
    Resources to Help You Take Your Playing Further 142
    About the Author 145

Introduction

Welcome to The Missing Method's songwriter's journal! In this book you'll find the space you need to jot down song ideas as they come to you.

How this book is designed

We've created this book to give you the space to create with the tools we have found useful. Therefore, the first 30 pages is just for lyrics, ideas, notes, or whatever else you may want to write down. After that, you'll find 50 pages of blank staff paper organized in 12 groups, each preceded by a page for writing out chords and lyrics. In the final section, you'll find more of the same, this time with guitar tablature instead of staff paper.

We've also left room on each staff and TAB page for adding your own chord symbols and lyrics as needed. And we've included a lined page at the beginning of the staff and TAB sections for you to jot general notes or create a contents list for that section.

More tools to assist your songwriting

More than just blank pages for songwriting, this book also includes a reference section. This includes basic chords, basic scales, common strum patterns, and information about some of our other books that may help you strengthen your skills, thereby improving your songwriting. You can find these and more at TheMissingMethod.com.

Don't forget to have fun

Like with all creative endeavors, writing songs is a process, and we hope that this book will help make that process easier for you and allow you to keep track of all your best ideas. Keep in mind that a-ha moments often come not when we try to force it, but when we give the mind a break.

Most of all, remember why you started writing: because of your love of music and the joy it brings.

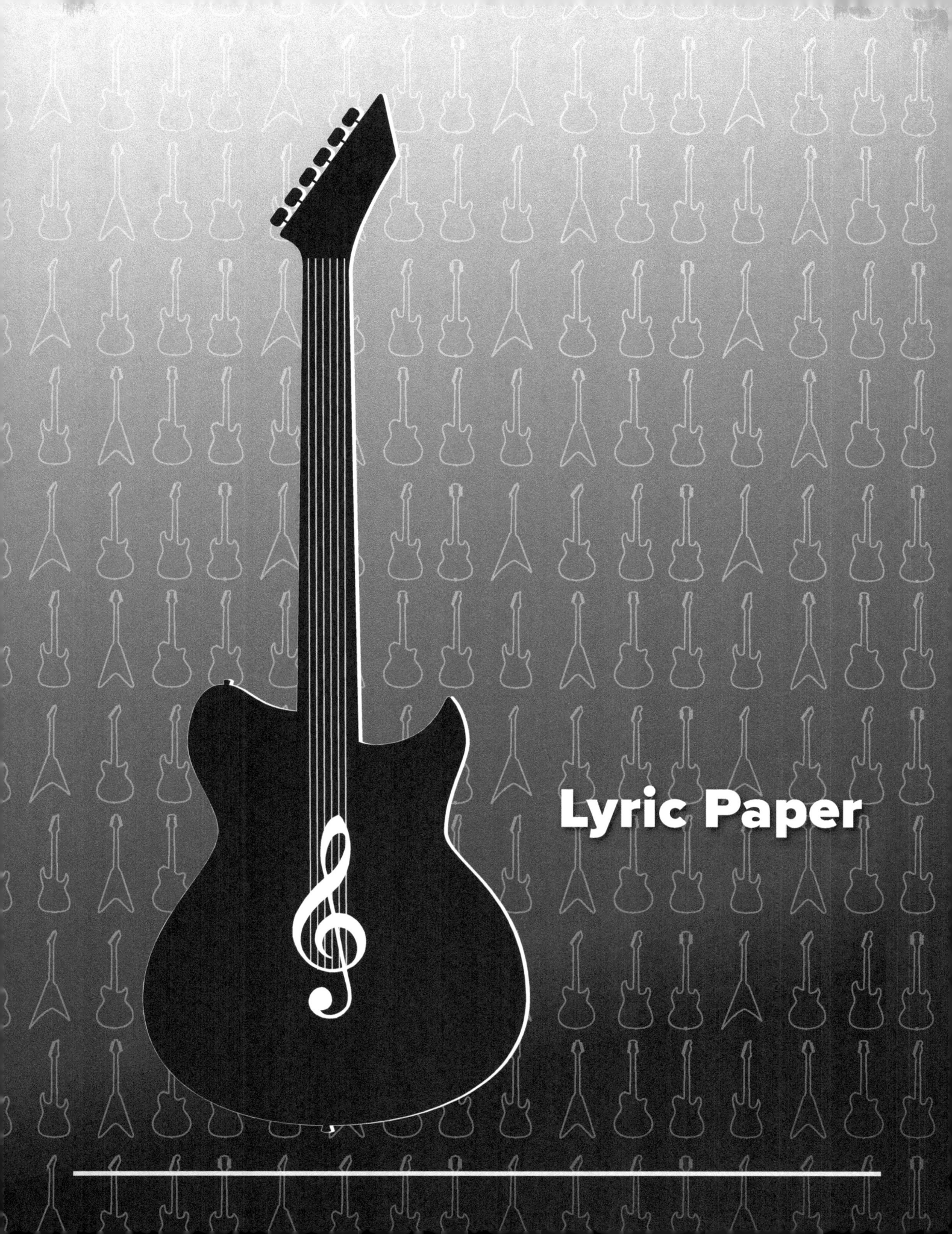

LYRIC PAPER

LYRIC PAPER

LYRIC PAPER

LYRIC PAPER

LYRIC PAPER

LYRIC PAPER

LYRIC PAPER

LYRIC PAPER

LYRIC PAPER

LYRIC PAPER

LYRIC PAPER

LYRIC PAPER

STAFF PAPER

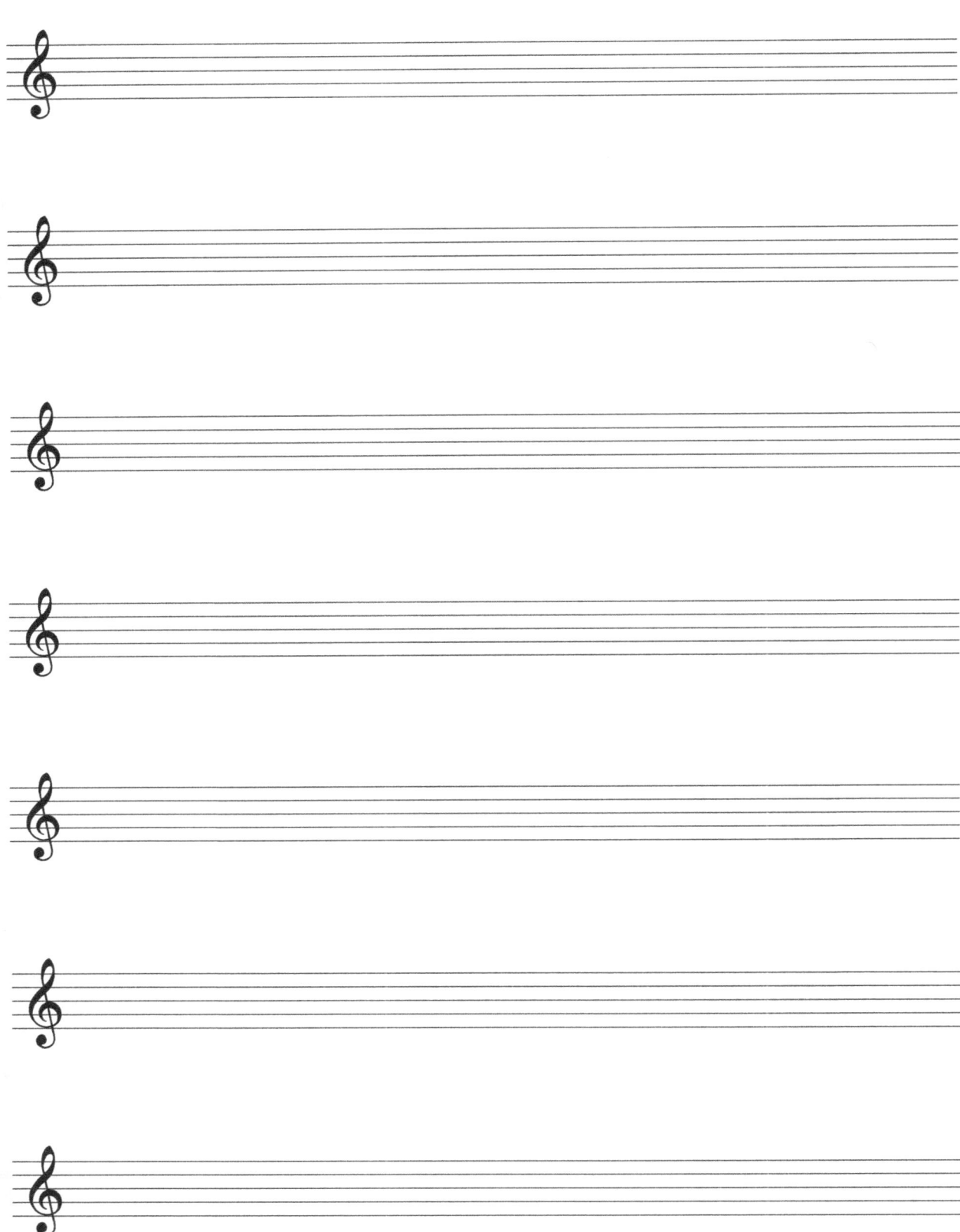

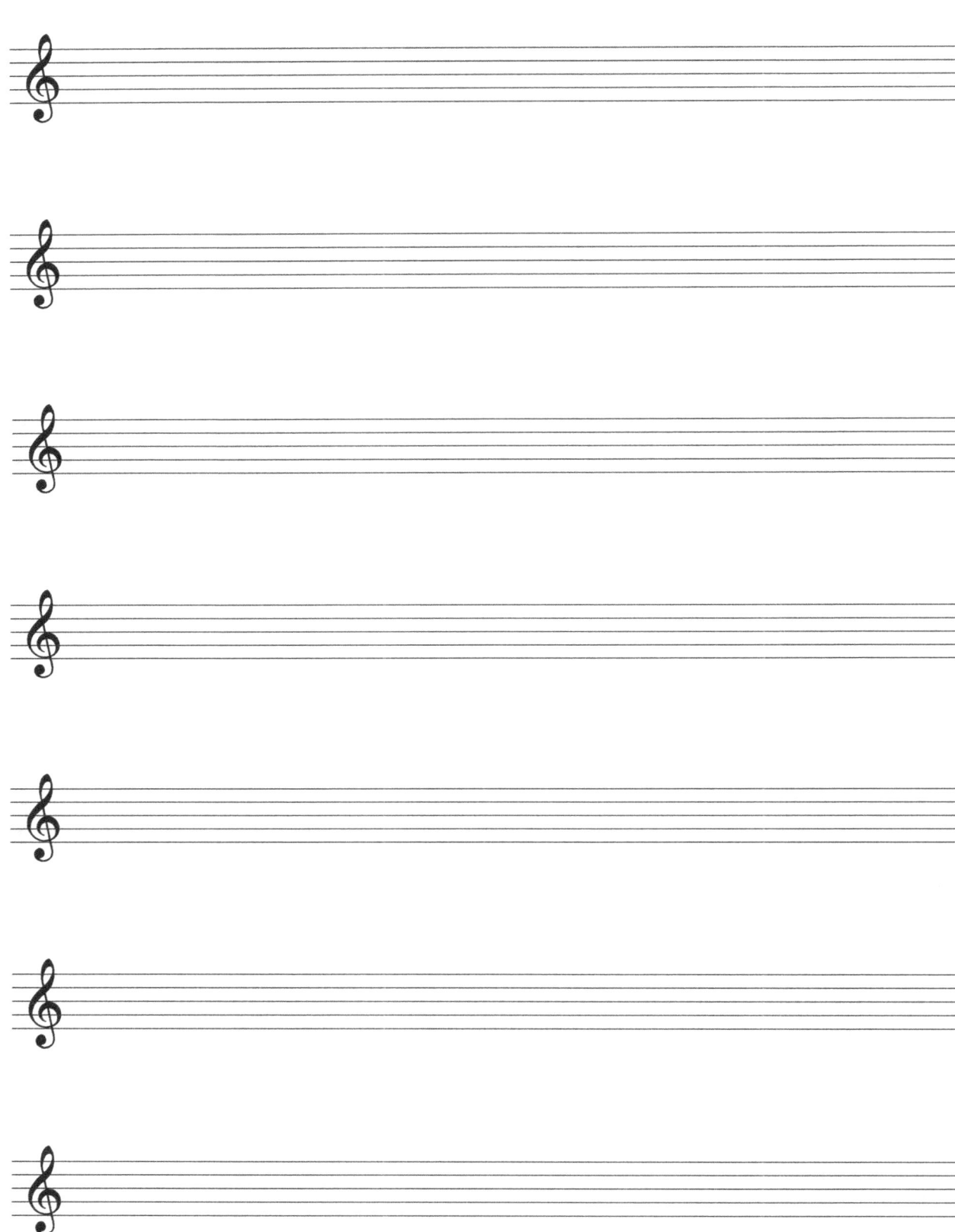

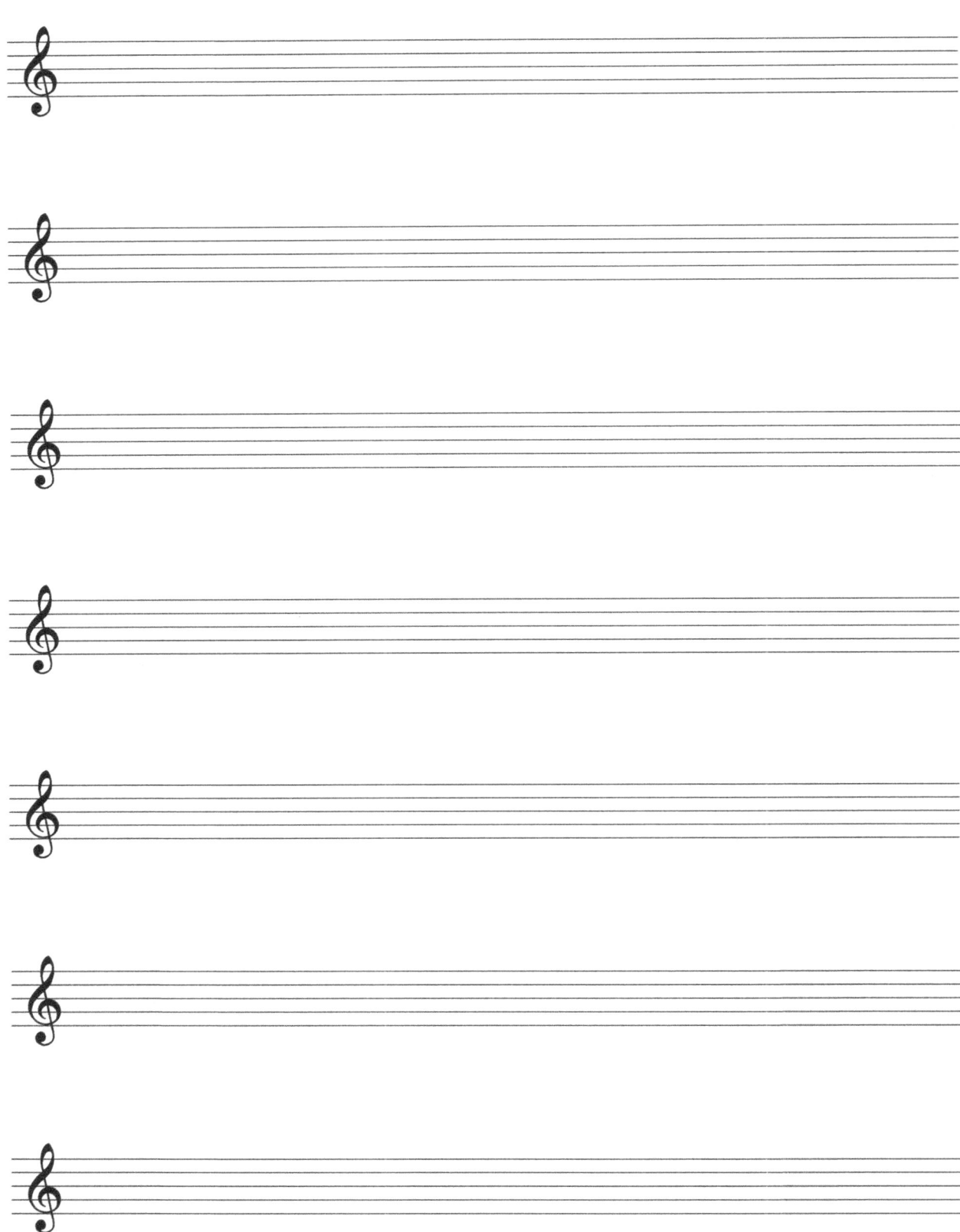

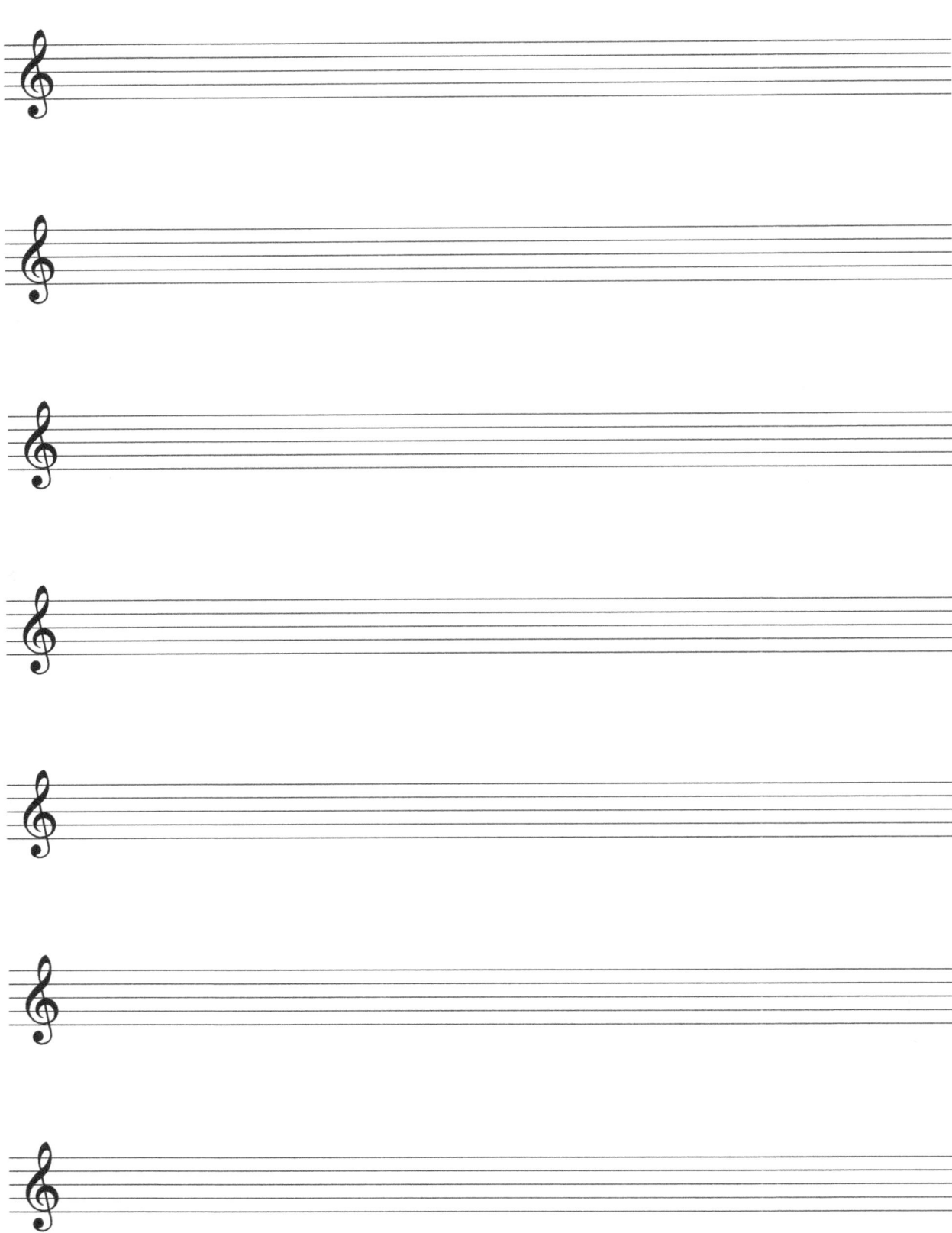

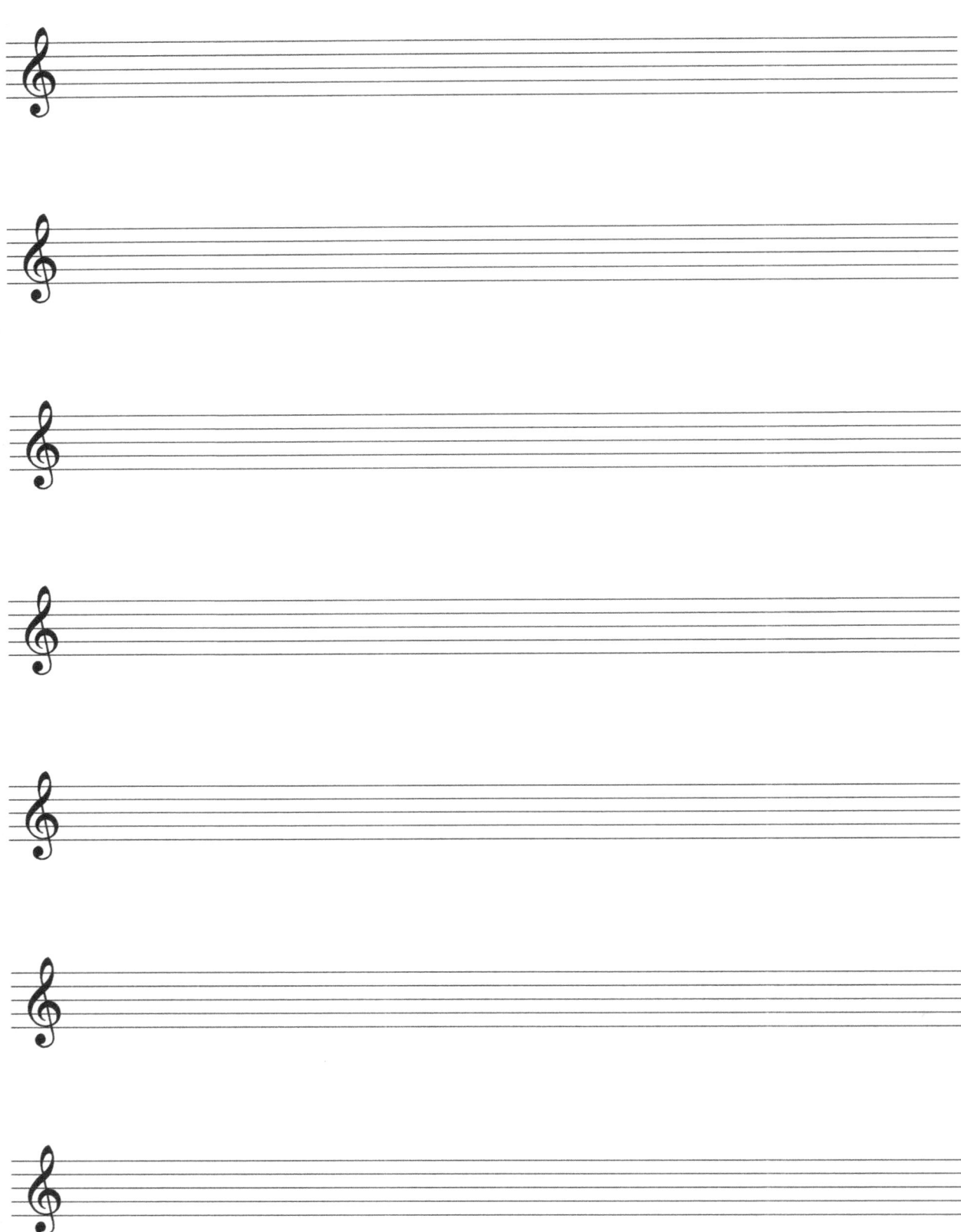

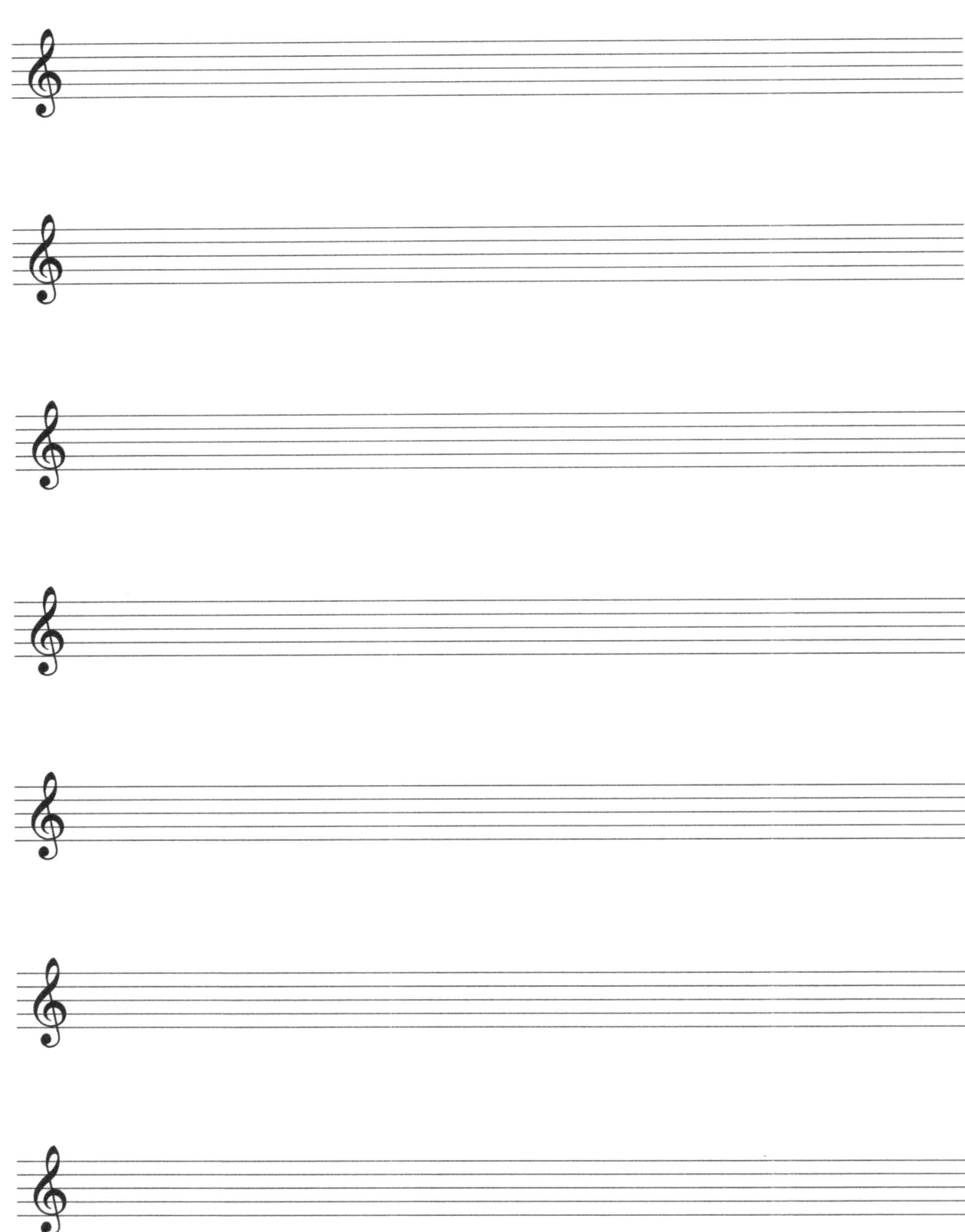

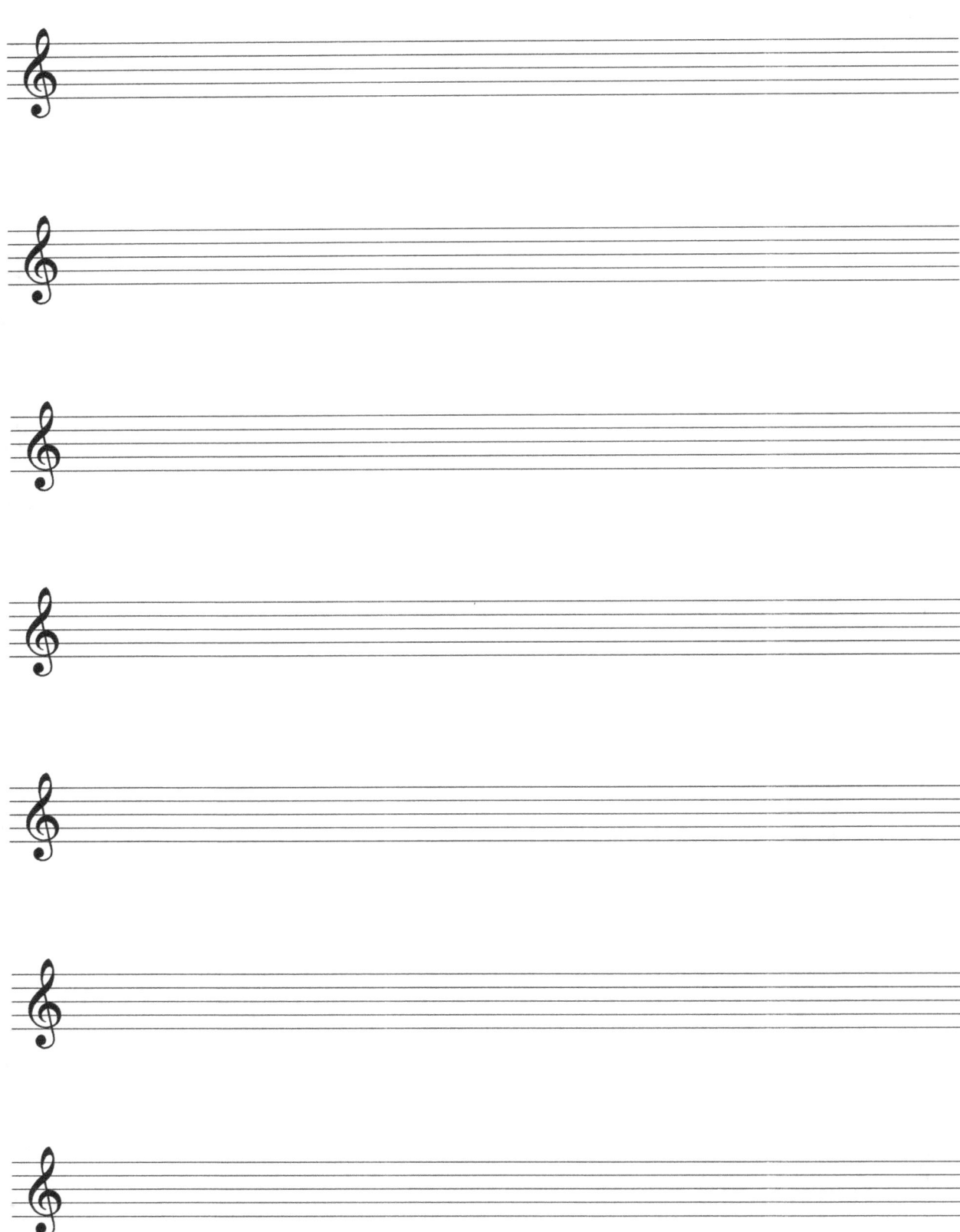

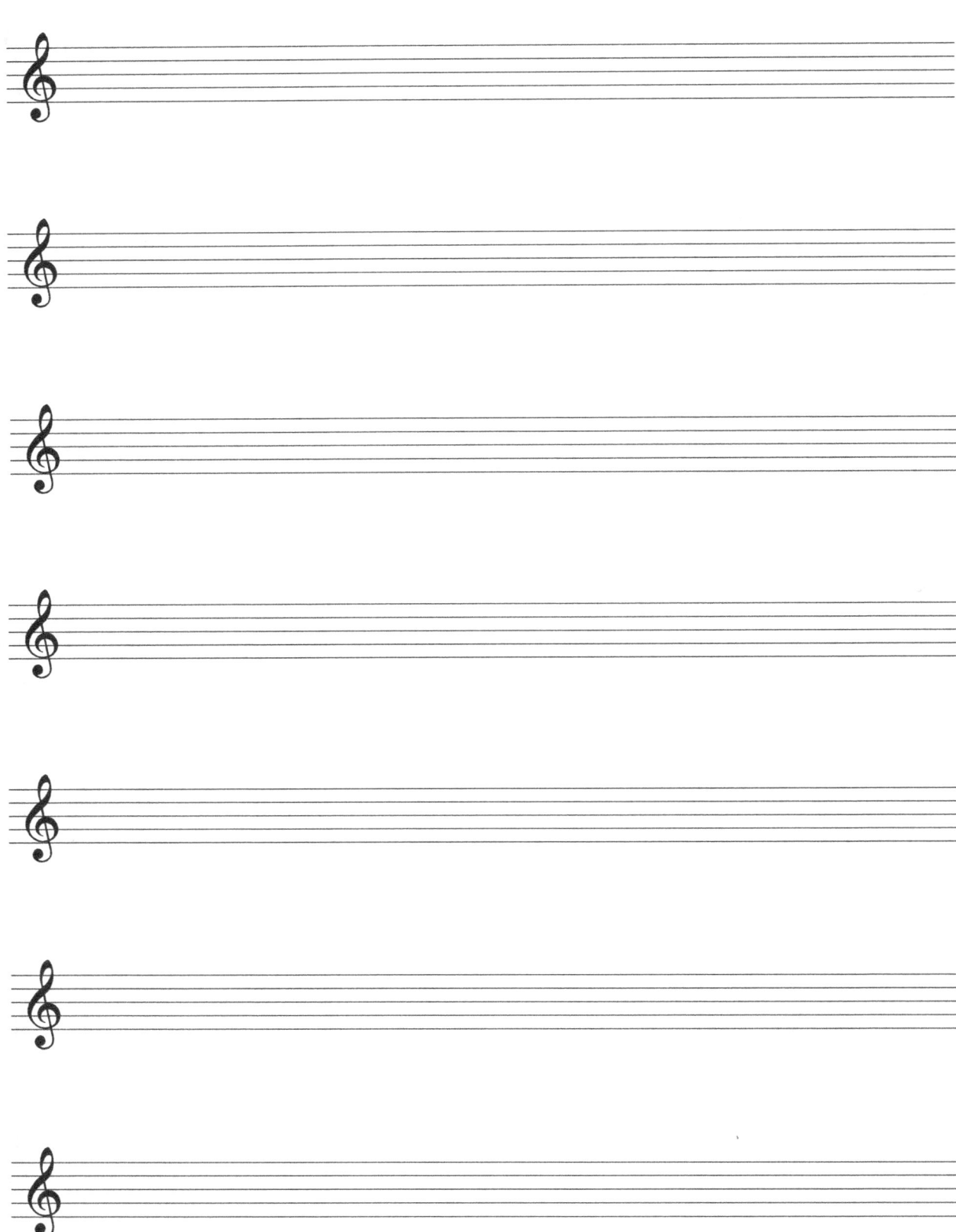

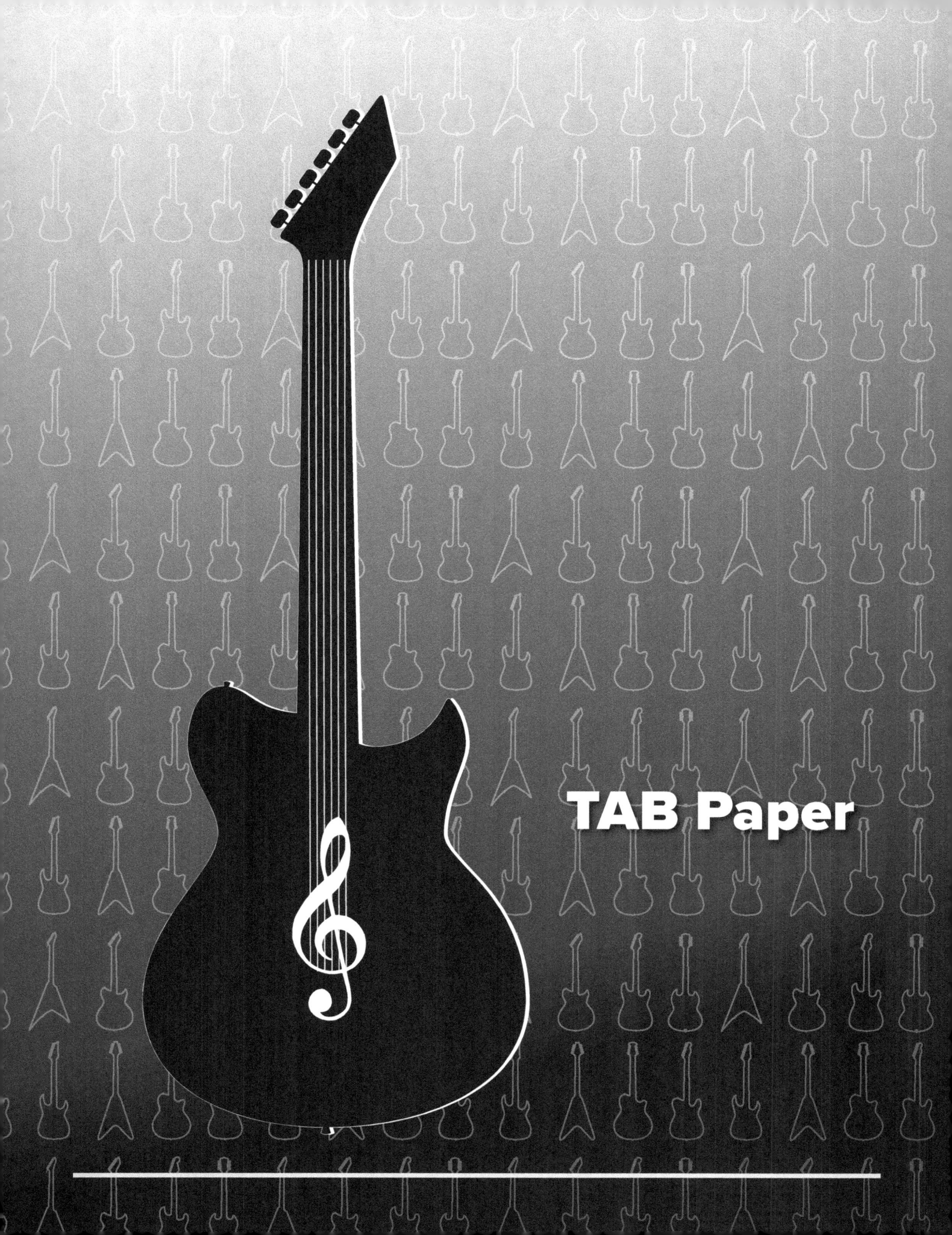

TAB PAPER

TAB PAPER

TAB PAPER

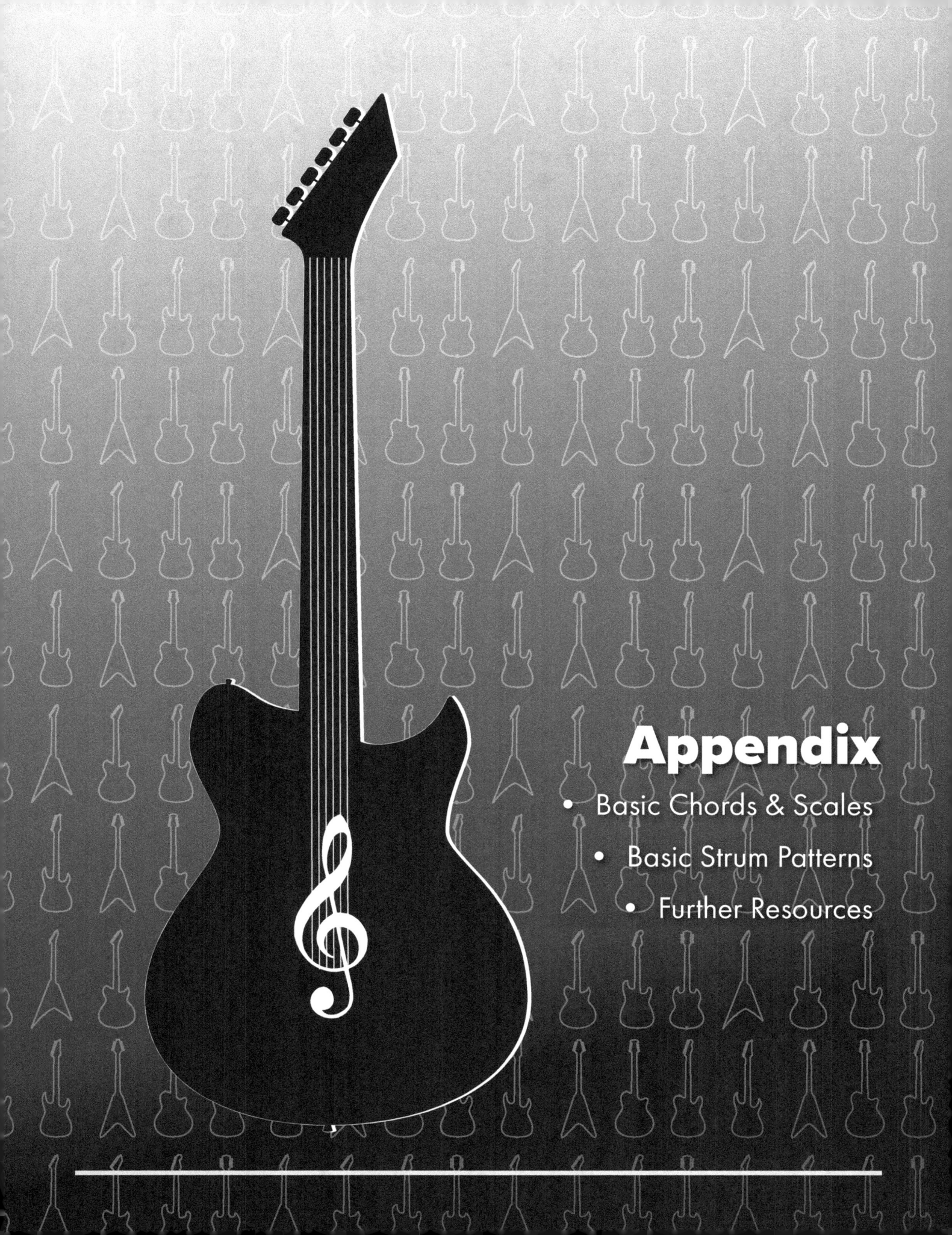

Basic Chords

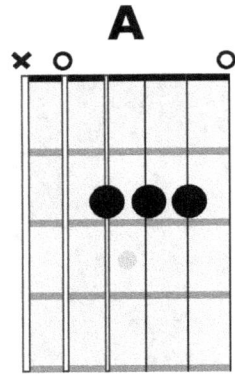 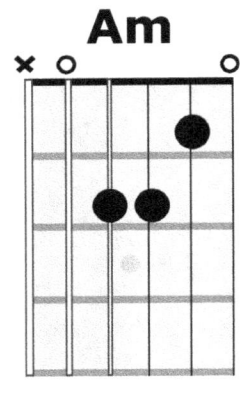 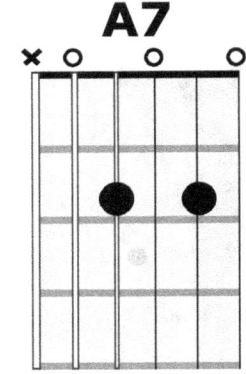 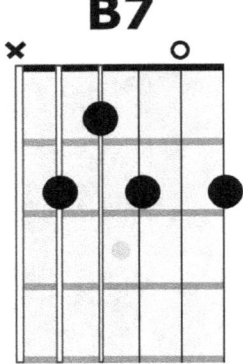

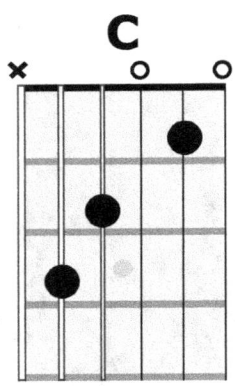 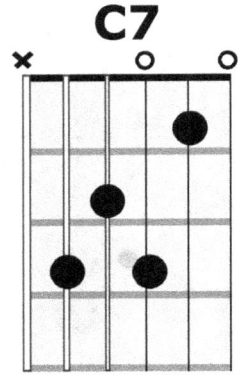 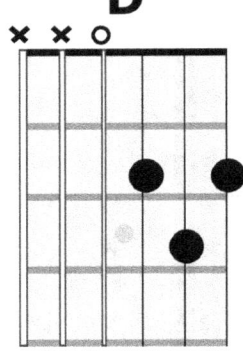 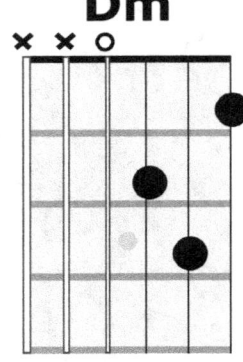

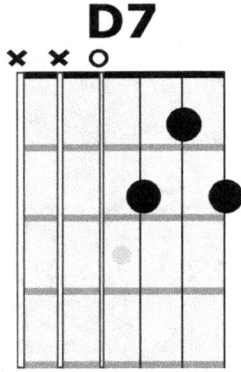 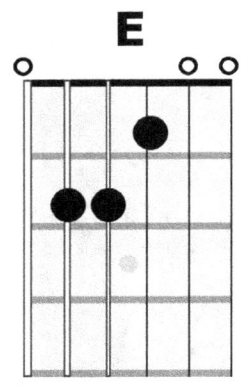 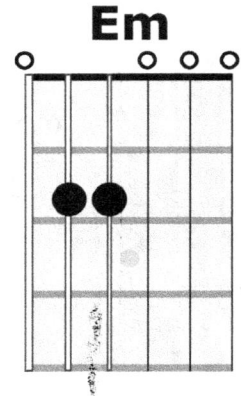 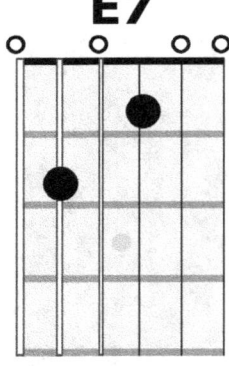

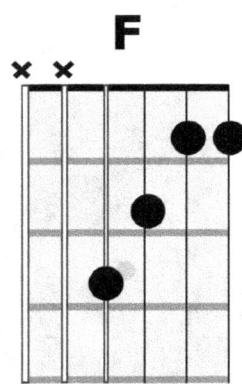 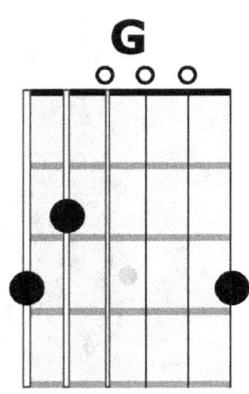 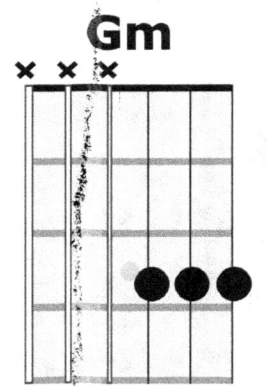 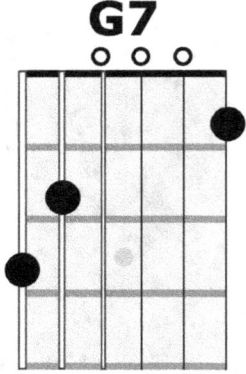

Basic Scales

Major Scale

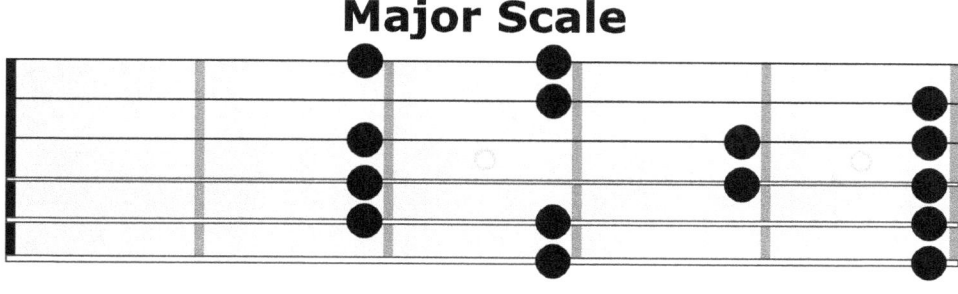

Natural Minor Scale

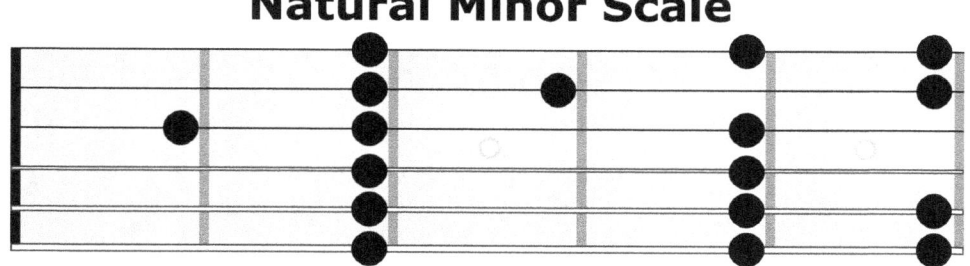

Harmonic Minor Scale

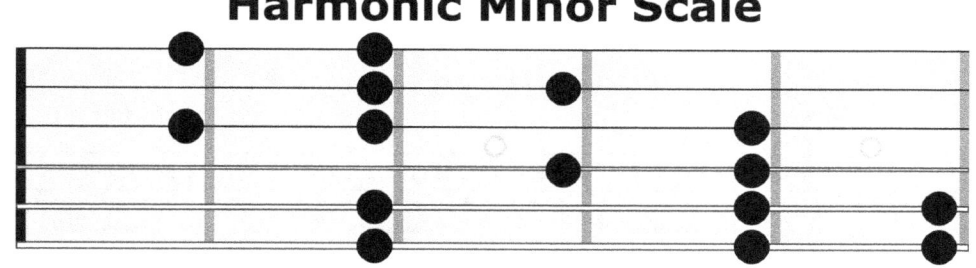

Minor Pentatonic Scale

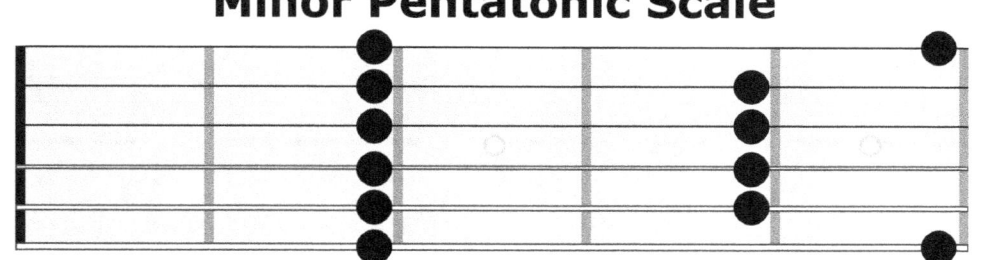

Major Pentatonic Scale

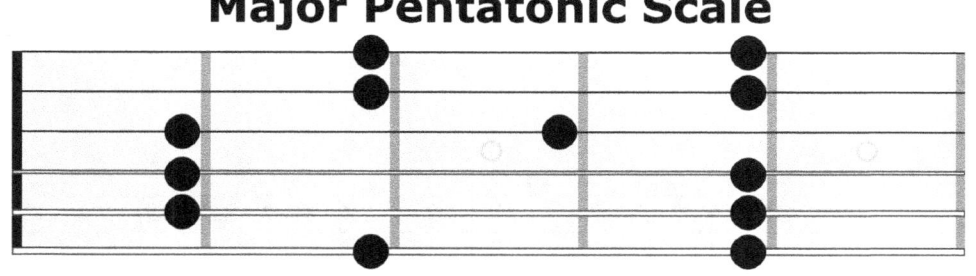

Common Strum Patterns

Patterns in 4/4 Time

138

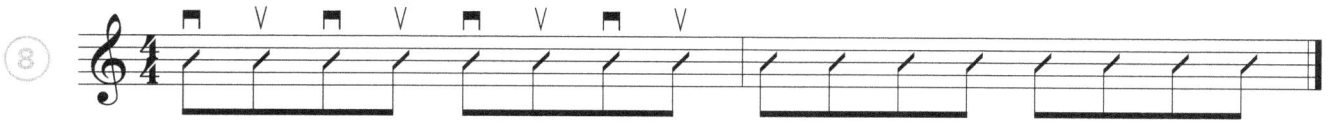
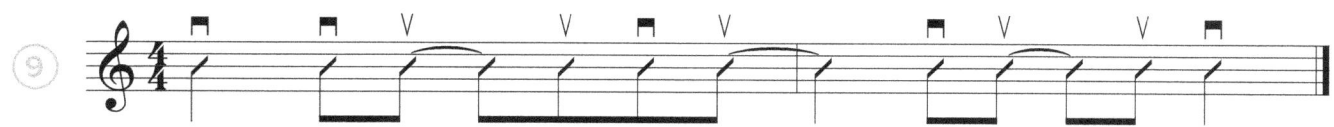

Patterns in 3/4 Time

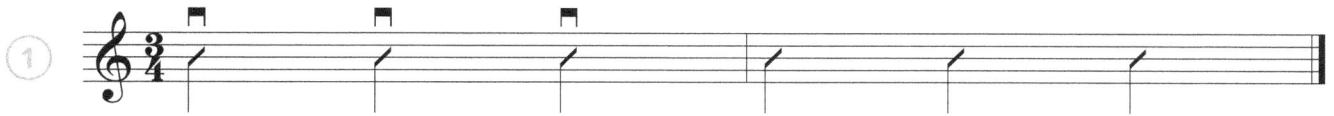
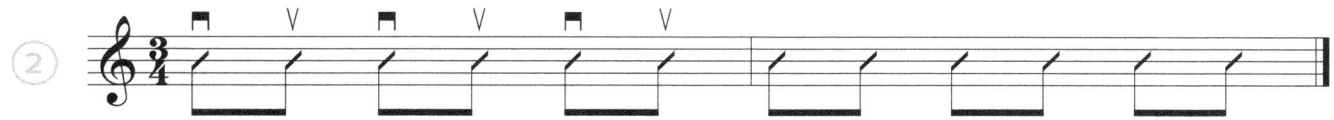
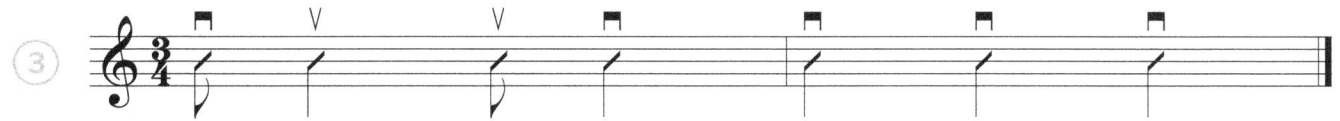
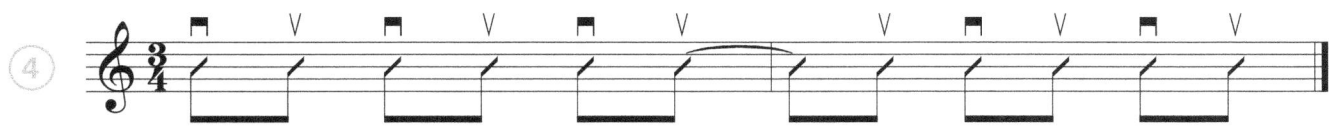
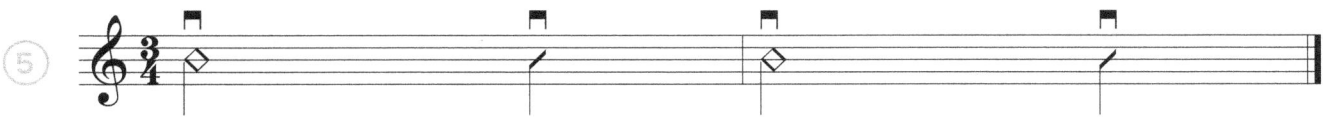

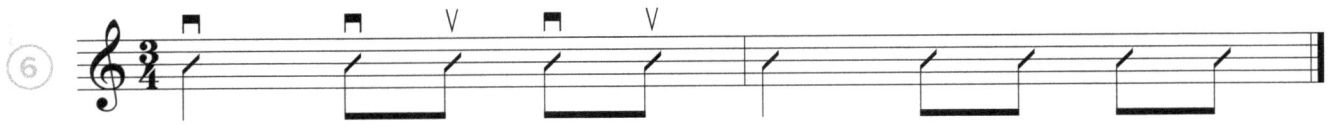

Patterns in 6/8 Time

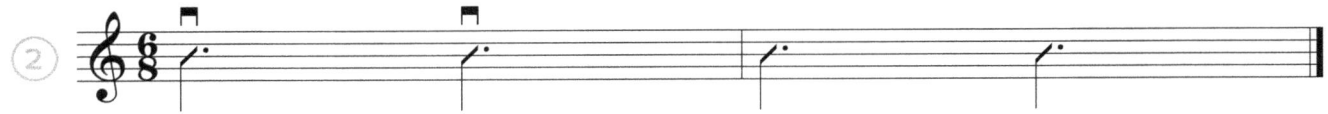

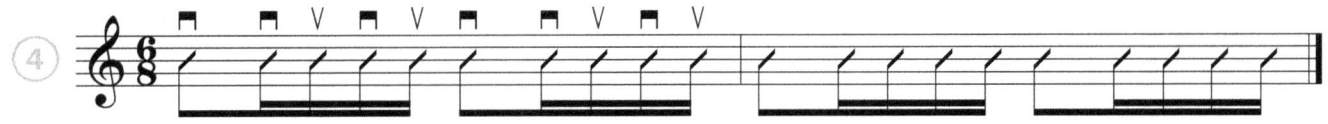

Patterns in 2/4 Time

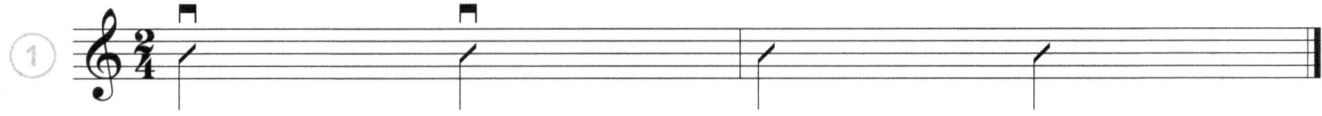

Resources to Help You Take Your Playing Further

Perfect Practice

Rethink how you practice. Stop practice burn-out. Learn the secrets to transforming your practice time into time well-spent. This book will help you to figure out how to identify and overcome the obstacles in your way by showing you what to practice and how to structure your time so you see results faster.

Guitar Chord Master Series

Guitar Chord Master is the only method book series that focuses exclusively on learning chords and strum patterns. Each book takes you step-by-step through the process of learning chords in a musical context, allowing you to master them for life! The series covers open chords, power chords, barre chords, how to use a capo, moveable shapes, and much more. Available in right and left-handed editions.

Technique Master Series

 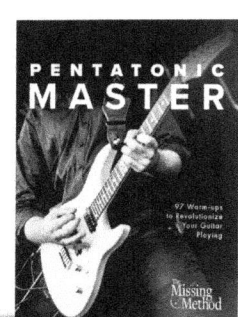

Avoid injury and learn how to play the right way with The Technique Master Series. Book 1 gets you started by helping you focus on basic techniques that build strength and dexterity, while focusing on time and efficiency. Book 2: Pentatonic Master continues to help you develop your technique while you learn to play the pentatonic scale all over the neck. Discover the difference a good set of warm-ups can make!

The Missing Method for Guitar Note Reading Series

Designed with the serious guitar player in mind, The Missing Method for Guitar Note Reading series teaches you how to read every note on the guitar, from the open strings to the 22nd fret. If you are looking to master the fretboard, this is the series for you! Available in right and left-handed editions.

Find these and more at TheMissingMethod.com.

APPENDIX

About the Author

Christian J. Triola holds a Bachelor's Degree in Music (Jazz Studies) and a Master's Degree in Education, both from The University of Akron. He has taught guitar, bass, mandolin, ukulele, and piano for over 20 years, is the author of over two dozen guitar method books, and has played in a variety of bands in addition to his many solo performances.

What is the Missing Method?

The Missing Method™ is an imprint of Tenterhook Books, LLC, owned and operated by Christian J. Triola and his wife, Amy Joy Triola. The imprint began in 2013 in an effort to bring method books that didn't exist to Christian's guitar students. Today, we have expanded that mission to create high quality instructional materials to inspire and empower guitar players around the world. The Missing Method now spans many series of guitar books, addressing topics from chords, to note reading, practice strategies, playing techniques and much more.

Learn more and join our growing community at TheMissingMethod.com.

www.ingramcontent.com/pod-product-compliance
Lightning Source LLC
Chambersburg PA
CBHW081747100526
44592CB00015B/2334